The Old and New Legends of

Murrells Inlet, South Carolina

Tales of the South Strand

By Christine Vernon

Illustrations by Christine Vernon

THE OLD AND NEW LEGENDS OF MURRELLS INLET, SOUTH CAROLINA

First edition. January 8, 2021.

ISBN: 979-8201408541

Written by Christine Vernon.

Table of Contents

To my mother and father who have passed on to the spirit world...I thank you for encouraging me to be a storyteller and help me to find my passion in life. Thanks to my husband Paul who also loves a good story.

Acknowledgements

Many thanks to my husband, Paul Vernon, who introduced me to the legends and lore from our previous storytellers of the inlet. Reading the tales of Clarke A. Willcox and Genevieve 'Sister' C. Peterkin inspired me to carry on their work to pass on our history and legends to others. It also encouraged me to continue researching the history behind the legends and update some of our local lore.

To my family, especially my mother who always gave in and bought me books on local ghosts and legends and encouraged me to read.

To friends and neighbors, Tom Hora and the Chandler family for allowing me to sit on your back porch by the marsh and listen in on family memories of life at the Hermitage.

To Chief Hatcher of the Waccamaw Tribe. A wonderful storyteller himself.

Thanks to my friend, Shane Gage for spending hours with me exchanging stories regarding Pawleys Island lore.

Thanks to the Murrells Inlet/South Strand community and all my tour guests who have supported my ghost/history walk over the years.

I am very appreciative to the owners,management and staff of the Lazy Gator Gift Shop for allowing me to host my tours on your front porch. And to all the locals and visitors I have met on that porch who have generously shared their ghost stories with me.

Finally, to the wonderful owners,staff and patrons along the Murrells Inlet MarshWalk. You have welcomed me with open arms, especially Mr. Al Hitchcock of Drunken Jack's Restaurant. Thank you for encouraging me to carry on our legends and history.

Preface

In my life, there have always been two loves. The first is the arts. I have been a full-time artist since I could hold a pencil. When I was very young, my parents or other family members would ask me what I wanted to be when I grew up. I would respond,"I AM an artist!" My second love is storytelling. Not just any stories. Mostly, ghost stories. I have always believed in spirits, ghosts, and entities since childhood. Not only did I believe, I saw and felt them as well. I would see them in all forms: mists, glowing orbs, or full apparitions. Mostly, I could feel their presence. I knew they were all around me. Being raised Catholic, however, you didn't discuss ghosts. You believed what the nuns taught you. You either went to heaven or hell. Or, God forbid, purgatory if you hadn't been baptized. Period.

I grew up in a large family of 5 sisters and 2 brothers near Philadelphia, Pa. Nearly every summer my family would go camping. Mostly to the same campground in the center of the state, but on occasion, we would head south to North Carolina to the Outer Banks. Yes, the 'Graveyard of the Atlantic'. I loved spending time on the Albemarle Sound with my parents and their friends. I'd watch the locals catch crabs and as the tide went out, I would see the shells of old wooden boats that had sailed years before peeking out from their watery graves. But most of all, I loved spending time in local tourist gift shops looking at the books that told of the local area legends and lore. I would beg my parents to buy me these books. It didn't matter where we went or what the stories may be about...I had to have those books. I would inhale the stories. Memorize them all. And, whenever a situation presented itself, I would recite what I had learned to my family.

Some of my favorite memories of childhood were sitting around the campfire or the kitchen table at our family farm and listening to my father or mother tell the stories of our family history or local folktales. Everyone had their favorite story to tell, but mine were the ghost stories.

It was my job. My calling. When you've seen or felt them around as much as I have, you want to find out more. Why are they here? Where did they come from? Was there a hidden history to each of these tales? Just how did the legend get started?

Each time I heard a new ghost story, I would try to research just where it all started. But, life would get in the way and when I grew into adulthood, my full-time job and raising a child would be first and foremost. My love of storytelling would be put up on the shelf, along with all those dusty ghost books I had collected as a child.

But, when I was hitting my 40's, I left the snowy winters of Pennsylvania for the warmer climate of South Carolina. I moved down with my first husband...and ended up with a second. It happens. But my second husband, Paul Vernon would be the one who would encourage me to investigate the local lore and legends of the South Strand. He had lived here long enough to have met and befriended the previous storyteller, Clarke A. Willcox. Clarke owned the Hermitage, the most haunted plantation home in Murrells Inlet. At least, according to him. Later, I would learn the stories told by Genevieve C. Peterkin. Otherwise known as Sister Peterkin. But, with their passing, Paul and I felt that the history and legends were being lost. So, I decided to start a local ghost/history tour to tell the stories to anyone who would listen. Many who come along on my walks are the tourists to the marsh. Many of them had stories to tell about their hometowns, too. What I enjoyed was having the locals come to me and tell me what they knew about the local lore and what their personal experiences were. And, for this, I am grateful. Not many wish to come forward to tell about their frightening encounters. They don't wish to be ridiculed by their neighbors and friends.

I perform my ghost and history tours out on the MarshWalk in Murrells Inlet. The MarshWalk, itself is not haunted, but the old plantation homes and beaches of the area are. The MarshWalk is a very small boardwalk that connects a number of restaurants each having fabulous, coastal views of the marsh and its wildlife. Murrells Inlet is also known as 'The Seafood Capital of South Carolina'. The restaurants own that title. Each restaurant has a wide variety of fresh fish of the day caught by our local fishermen. Yes, we are still a fishing village. The restaurants offer other seasonal favorites such as blue crabs or oysters. They say deep-fried cornmeal called hushpuppies were invented here, too. But, the history of the inlet goes much further than that.

Native American tribes lived along the coast for many generations. According to the chief of the local Waccamaw Tribe, Murrells Inlet is their tribal cemetery. The Waccamaw called Murrells Inlet area 'Wachesaw'...'the place of great weeping'. A few of the burial mounds of the Waccamaw have been excavated and the bones of these great people have been taken to local museums for study. The Waccamaw hope to one day receive the bones of their ancestors back so they may be buried according to their traditions.

It is said in 1526, the Spanish settled just south of Murrells Inlet long before other Europeans but did not stay long. Pirates would use the coast as a hideout and eventually, the British, Irish, and others would settle here and raise indigo and rice. We were originally called 'Murray's Inlet' on old maps dating back to the 1700s. I could not find anyone named Murray in that time period, but there was a man named Murrell (also spelled Morrall). He purchased over 2,400 acres in our vicinity. According to another historian, Murrells' name had been spelled differently on a few documents. In Early American history, many settlers were illiterate. Names would be spelled incorrectly often. Others say we were named after Captain John Murrell, the pirate, but I found no information he is our namesake. It wouldn't be until the early 1900s that the Postal Service would build a post office and officially name us 'Murrells Inlet'.

Some of the wealthiest plantation owners of the South owned plantations in Murrells Inlet. It would be a particular rice called 'Carolina Gold' that would make everyone wealthy. Thus, the beginning of our long and very interesting history would emerge from the incredibly difficult life of all those who had to endure brutal summer heat and mosquito-ridden swamps.

So I would say our little fishing village has several stories and secrets to tell. Everyone has a story or two. We all, for the most part, believe our family secrets will go with us to our graves. The sins of the father (or mother) will come back to, excuse the pun, haunt us. But, not everything can be buried forever. So, if you don't want your secrets told, I suggest you live a good, wholesome life. Or, keep your skeletons from falling out of your closet.

The following stories are the tales that have been handed down by the previous storytellers. The majority are about Murrells Inlet, and a couple stories are about small towns just south of us called Litchfield and Pawleys Island. Together we comprise what we call 'The South Strand'. Some of these tales have been updated from my interviews with people who have recently experienced these unusual phenomena for themselves. Remember, every storyteller has their version of the events. Some tell the tales taller than the oak trees around here. Others, tell it the way it was handed down to them word for word. Myself...I love regaling the best of them all. That is, of course, what storytelling is all about. Making your tales taller than the last storytellers.

The Story of Alice Belin Flagg

I am constantly being asked who lies beneath the burial stone marked "ALICE " in All Saints Cemetery in Pawleys Island. Some say it is Alice Belin Flagg. She was the sister of Dr. Allard Flagg, owner of the Wachasaw Plantation. Alice, her mother and Dr. Flagg lived at the family home called the Hermitage. So, I will start with this legend first. After all, it is our favorite ghost story here in Murrells Inlet. And, the one I tell the most on my ghost and history tour.

In 1849, Reverend James Belin owned a rice plantation called Wachasaw in Murrells Inlet. An unusual name for a plantation for in the language of the local Waccamaw Indians who lived on this land, Wachasaw means 'the place of great weeping." Reverend Belin never had children of his own. So, he decided to give a large portion of his plantation to his nephew, Dr. Allard Flagg as a wedding gift. Along with the land, Dr. Flagg also inherited the Hermitage, a beautiful summer home along the banks of the marsh. Many plantation owners built their summer homes along the beaches and coastline to get away from the mosquitos and enjoy a cool ocean breeze.

Dr. Flagg asked his widowed mother and his little sister, Alice, to come and live with him. Alice, we believe, was 15 years old at the time. But, soon, Alice would start a romance with a local man who was working in the turpentine industry. Dr. Allard was against this courtship. The Flaggs were very wealthy rice plantation owners and thought this gentleman was beneath their standing. When the gentleman would come to court Alice, it is said Dr. Flagg would ride in the carriage with his sister and make her suitor ride a horse beside them. Dr. Flagg would do anything to keep his sister away from her beau.

So, to end the romance, Dr. Flagg sent poor Alice to Charleston to boarding school. Alice did not like Charleston. She enjoyed the country life and of course, being with her beau. It is said he would secretly continue to court her on occasion at the school.

One day, the school contacted Dr. Flagg. Alice had taken ill. Whether it was malaria or another malady such as yellow fever(country fever) is unknown, but her temperature was dangerously high. Dr. Flagg drove his horse and carriage to Charleston, which in those times took days to cover the hazardous terrain. By the time he brought Alice back to the Hermitage, she was unconscious and on death's doorstep.

He picked Alice up and took her to her upstairs bedroom. As he laid her down in bed, he noticed something around her neck. It was a ribbon. And upon that ribbon was a ring. And not just any ring. She got secretly engaged to the local turpentine salesman. Dr. Allard was outraged. And, legend has it....he took the ring off her neck and threw it into the marsh behind the home.

He went back to Alice's room to check on her and found her awake and crying. "Where is my ring?" she asked. And he told her what he had done with it.

"Please," she cried," "please find my ring." But he and the household staff knew it was gone forever. Alice would die a few nights later in her room.

After her death, it is said, she was buried in the backyard of the home just a few feet away from where the ring had been tossed into the marshy water. Her mother was out of town when her daughter passed. Alice had to be buried behind the Hermitage until her mother came home. When the mother returned, she had Alice's body exhumed and buried, some say, in All Saints Cemetery in Pawleys Island just south of Murrells Inlet. However, All Saints Cemetery records tell us that Alice Flagg is not buried there. Church documents say she was buried in the area named Cedar Hill which is now Belin Methodist Cemetery. That is the land Reverend James Belin owned. Unfortunately, no one knows exactly where her final resting place is in the cemetery because her grave is unmarked. Her stone could have been swept away due to flooding, a regular occurrence here on the coast.

This is why so many people go to All Saints Cemetery in Pawleys Island. If you go to cemetery, you will find a huge, marble slab on the ground in the family plot. It has only one word on it... ALICE. Some say the stone is a memorial to Alice's Aunt, who was buried in another cemetery. But, when I saw the All Saints Church burial records, I came across something. In 1893, another Alice Flagg would meet her end.

Locals say it was the day "the ocean met the river'. A tidal wave came across what is known as Magnolia Beach (Huntington Beach State Park) and made its way through Murrells Inlet with such force, it swept away many of the occupants. Most of all, the Flagg family. This is why we call it 'The Flagg Flood."

I read the names of those who drowned in the flood. It is said most of the Flaggs and a couple of family friends were washed away. But looking again, I noticed there were two names listed on the same line of the deceased. It listed Dr. A.B. (Dr. Arthur Belin) and 'Little Alice Flagg'.

Other children who were swept away were listed as 'infant' or 'child' on the church's register of the dead. But, this is the only reference of any child being named 'little'. Little Alice Flagg was 4 years old when she was swept away by the waters. Her full name was Alice Rutledge Flagg. There is a memorial stone at All Saints with the names of those who perished on October 13, 1893. But the stone in All Saints that has the single name 'Alice' upon it could be a memorial stone to any one of the many Alice Flaggs who lived here on the Waccamaw Neck. Dr. Allard Flagg named his newborn daughter Alice Flagg in 1850. And, so did another Flagg relative. Normally, most gravestones would have both birth and death dates upon them. But this one does not.

From the stories told by Clarke Willcox and Sister Peterkin, Alice Flagg haunted the Hermitage, although Sister Peterkin called her the 'lady in white'. Yes, The Hermitage still stands, but not in its original plot by the marsh. Relatives moved the home...just around the corner from my own house. And, in speaking with them, they have told me of their close calls with her specter. It is said one relative watched a hairbrush fly off a vanity table and across Alice's room. Even Sister Peterkin tells of she and her mother having a close encounter with the young spirit.

I go past Alice's family home quite often. And, I wave to her and wish her well. And, I wish she would stay there, too. I receive enough visits from spirits and I don't need another visiting me during the night, thank you very much.

Locals say Alice not only haunts her family home, but also, the marsh where her home once stood, still going through the marsh grass looking for her ring. The area where the Hermitage once stood is now a small, gated neighborhood of many modern homes.

One night while doing my ghost tour, a gentleman pulled me aside and told me he just recently moved into the neighborhood. He also informed me that Alice had come by his home one night. Seems she was curious about this newcomer and rapped on his window as if to say hello. When he went to look for her, she was gone.

But, I have come to a conclusion why Alice Belin Flagg haunts All Saints Cemetery even though she is not buried there. If you were to go there, you will find small trinkets and dozens of little plastic rings left on the marble stone. Folks from everywhere place rings on the stone because we feel so sad that Alice was unable to find her engagement ring in life, we leave them for her in death.

I have always asked the folks who accompany me on my tours not to go to our cemeteries and talk to the dead. If the dead want to talk to you, they can find you quite easily no matter where you are. And, how would you like it if people came to your grave after your passing and kept asking you to wake up and talk to them? I would probably find it a little annoying. But, lastly...you may think you are in the cemetery talking to

Alice Belin Flagg, but you may wake up her neighbor. And he may take a fancy to you ...and follow you home.

Drunken Jack

Pirates. Yes, one of my favorite subjects. Probably because I am the Pirate Lady of Murrells Inlet. I am listed on The International Pirate Directory, too. But, being a modern-day pirate doesn't come with a ship or treasure, unfortunately. More or less, I have a jon boat that leaks and a lot of plastic doubloons that I hand out to local children on the MarshWalk. But, that's not why I took on this persona. If you want to attract business, then be attractive. And, dressing as a pirate (and let me reiterate ...a pirate, not a wench) gets me noticed. Folks approach me and ask me why I dress in costume. This opens up a dialogue and allows me to pass on some of our lore and legends. And maybe, recommend a good place to eat, too. Murrells Inlet is the ' Seafood Capital of South Carolina' after all.

I regale stories of a mix of both history and legends during my walks and lectures. One of our most famous tales here on the South Strand is about one particular pirate. And, his name is Jack. There have been a couple of renditions of this story. Some say it was Blackbeard and his men who ventured on our shores. Another storyteller claims it was Captain Kidd who buried his treasure here. Having looked at both options, I believe Blackbeard is the most likely of suspects. He loved the Carolina shores, especially North Carolina. Well, until he met his doom there.

First and foremost, I must say one historical fact. It was very rare for any pirate to bury treasure. The minute a pirate crew had anything of value in their hands, they would sail for the nearest port and spend their plunder on alcohol, women, and sometimes supplies. They spent it like you would your paycheck on a Friday night after a long hard week at the office...GONE! I believe pirates helped the local economies. Kind of like Robin Hoods of the sea. But, let's get back to Jack.

Legend has it, the pirates had just gotten back from the Carribean. They had stolen 32 barrels of rum and a treasure chest. They came across a small island near what is now Huntington Beach State Park. They decided to bury the treasure...and most of the rum. Of course, they opened a few barrels to celebrate their good fortune. So, the pirates were up most of the night eating oysters, drinking rum, and having a jolly good time.

Especially one pirate. His name was Jack.

Jack loved his rum. Maybe a little too much?! For, it is said, he passed out under some bushes on the island. The next morning, when Jack awoke from his drunken stupor, he looked around the island and no pirates! They left him behind. Now, what was poor old Jack supposed to do now? All he had was sand and seagulls and ...32 barrels of rum! I believe Jack was happy for a time on the little island.

It was hours before the pirates realized Jack was missing from the ship. But, they didn't seem to worry. They knew Jack could take care of himself. They would come back for Jack soon. Their idea of 'soon' turned into 1-½ years later! The pirates came back to the island but alas, no Jack. But they did find the bleached bones of a man, still clinging onto an empty rum bottle with his boney fingers. But, what could be even worse than that? No RUM! Well, of course, they didn't go back for Jack. They went back for the rum! But not only was the rum missing, but the treasure was gone as well. They say to this day folks still venture out to try their hand at locating the treasure, but no one has found anything...yet.

The island has changed quite a bit over the years and was named Drunken Jack's Island. A very fitting name. Now, whether poor pirate Jack haunts the area, I have not heard tell. The tides over the years have changed our coastline many times over. Hurricanes and floods, king tides and surges have created newer channels through the marsh and inlet. But, Drunken Jack's Island is still there. But, if you are ever out on your boat fishing for bluefish or red drum, take a look for old Jack. Tell him we still remember him fondly when we partake of libations.

On a side note, if you don't believe in the tale of Jack, you may believe this story as to how Drunken Jack Island was named. In the days before the Civil War, it is said there was a group of plantation owners who would gather together on the island and enjoy a feast of fish and brandy and brag of their great wealth from crops of indigo and rice. They called their little fest the 'Hot and Hot Fish Club' so named for the great quantities of cooked fresh fish they passed along to each other on huge platters.

I believe it was South Carolina Governor Robert F. W. Allston who spoke of a giant of a man who would eat his fill of fish at their club. His name was Jack Green. He was 6' 4" tall and weighed approximately 300 lbs. He was known to eat a great number of fish including the bones and drank quarts of brandy. By the time the meal was over, Jack would stumble out of the makeshift club building and pass out in the reeds on the island. It would take many men to move him, but on occasion, they would leave the giant Jack alone to sleep off his feast. So it looks like we may have another reason to name the island Drunken Jack's.

So, is it the giant Jack who haunts the island? No. I haven't heard of a particular person's spirit floating about. But, that doesn't mean someone isn't walking the beach and taking part in a farewell pint. It seems this island is a fitting place for just that.

The Grey Man

There are many, many different renditions of the Grey Man story. For one, the spelling of the word grey. I have seen it with an 'e' and an 'a'. So please, do not correct my spelling. I simply like using 'e' better.

One version tells of 2 men both in love with the same girl. One of the men was named Enoch Arden. He left to go overseas but before leaving became engaged to a girl from Pawleys Island. He would be gone for years and there was talk that his ship had sunk and he lost his life. Enoch's friend after hearing the news professed his love to the girl and they arranged to be married. On their wedding day, an unexpected guest arrived. A young man rode up on horseback. It was Enoch. The young man's ship had sunk, but his life was spared and he was able to make his way back to Pawleys. But, when he saw his fiance' had married another, he rode away towards the beach and ended his life in the ocean.

Another rendition says a young girl had married another man after she feared her true love was dead. Many months later, a ship crashed upon a reef off Pawleys Island. The young girl went to the beach and she found a young man who washed ashore and laid dying. She realized it to be the boy she was in love with years earlier but thought dead. After his passing, it is said he wanders Pawleys Island beach warning people of approaching hurricanes.

Still, others believe it is Percival Pawley, one of the first settlers on the Waccamaw Neck. He loved the island and after his death, his spirit returns to save us from violent storms. Others say it is Plowden C. J. Weston. He had owned the Pelican Inn which still stands to this day and has withstood many hurricanes over the years. But, if the first recorded sighting of the Grey Man was in 1822, then it couldn't be Weston, for he did not die until 1864.

I had read a story that named a couple who may be these famous lovers. The lady's name was Rachel Moore and her love was her cousin, Neville. Now, you must remember, back in the early plantation days it wasn't unheard of to fall in love and marry your cousin. But, Rachel Moore's family was against this union and sent Neville to Europe to study. The news came back that Neville had been challenged to a duel and died of his injuries. After some time, Rachel began to receive suitors. One was William Alston. They were soon married. Around 1778, Rachel was at their summer beach home when there was a knock on the door. When a servant opened the door, a disheveled, young man stood there. He told the servant his ship had wrecked offshore and he was sick and injured. He asked to see the head of the house and the servant retrieved the mistress. When Rachel entered the room and saw the young man, she fainted. It was Neville, her lost love. Neville realized that Rachel had married and in a rage, ran to the beach and into a terrible storm. He died just south of Pawleys Island, some say from a broken heart. So maybe it is Neville who comes back to the South Strand to save us from storm surges and hurricanes.

But, the following story is the rendition I love to tell:

The year was 1822. Young love! A boy and a girl from Pawleys Island wished to be married. But, the young man had to earn enough money before they could wed. So, he decided to leave South Carolina to make his fortune so they could marry. The young couple wrote love letters to each other throughout the year. In the late fall, she receives a letter from her love. He will be home in one month and they can be married. The young girl spends every waking hour preparing for the wedding. A month passes. She sends a servant with a horse to the river to meet her fiance's ship. When the young man sees his servant, he rushes off the ship, jumps on the horse, and gallops far ahead of the servant. He is so excited to be back home to see his love that he decides to take a shortcut through the marsh.

You never take a shortcut through the marsh! Ever! We have many dangerous things in our marsh. Poisonous snakes and alligators, too. But we also have something quite deadly just beneath our marsh waters. Pluff mud. It is similar to quicksand. If you are stuck in the pluff mud, it is nearly impossible to pull yourself out. The more you struggle, the more it pulls you in.

The horse raced into the mud and fell. The young man was thrown from his horse; his body slowly pulled under the grey mud. It was an hour later before the servant found his master, but it was too late. The servant then traveled back to the young girl's home and told her the unsettling news. The young girl cried out in disbelief. She ran from her home and dropped to her knees on the sandy shore. They say she spent days on the beach crying and praying to the Lord to bring back her love.

Then, one day, as she walked the beach, she noticed a man approaching her. He was dressed all in grey. The same color her love was wearing the day he died. The same color as the pluff mud that took his life. And, as he came close to her, she realized it was her love. He had come back! Maybe, she thought, he hadn't died but was only injured and now was here to marry her. So she ran to him with open arms and he stopped her in her tracks. He points inland and tells her that she and her family are in grave danger and must leave the island immediately. Then, disappears before her very eyes. She shakes her head in disbelief. She turns and runs back to her home and tells her family what she had witnessed. The family tries to console her. They believe the grief of losing her love has been too much for her to handle. But, then again, she never lied to them before and she was quite adamant about what she had seen. So they packed their bags and moved inland.

A few days later, the great hurricane of 1822 hit the South Carolina shore. The destruction was awful. Nearly every home sustained terrible damage or was washed away. But, not the young girl's home. It remained standing and virtually untouched by the storm.

That is the legend of the Grey Man. And, we take him very seriously, ya'll! He has appeared before every major hurricane to hit our coast. He was seen before Hurricane Hazel of 1954 and Hurricane Gracie of 1959. And, was seen before Hurricane Hugo of 1989. The devastation was incredible with Hugo. Damages in the tens of millions of dollars.

Homes especially in Garden City and Murrells Inlet were either flooded, washed off their foundations, or ripped apart by powerful winds. Except, I hear, for one family's beach home in Pawleys Island.

A family was staying at a beach home in Pawleys Island just before Hugo was to hit. Mr. and Mrs. 'M' we will call them were taking a stroll along the beach when a man in grey approached. Both had heard the story of the legendary Grey Man and looked at each other in awe at what they were witnessing. When they looked back towards the man, he was gone. They hurried back to their beach home, gathered their belongings, and took their family inland away from the coast. A few days later, Hurricane Hugo hit with incredible force. People were not allowed back to Pawleys Island until officials deemed it safe. When the family returned, their home was still standing, although homes to the left and right for miles around had been destroyed.

So, if you happen to be wandering along our beaches here on the South Strand and the winds begin to blow, the clouds darken and you see a man dressed in grey...RUN!

The Boo Hag

Now, I am not an expert on the tales of the Gullah Geechee. Many others have grown up in this culture who know the facts and history better than I. But, I tell this particular tale because of one little difference. I saw her. Not just saw...let's say, experienced her is more like it. In my own home in the middle of the night.

Now, I said earlier that I have seen or felt spirit(s) my whole life. Some in a good way. And a couple of others I wish I could forget. This is one of those times.

I had never heard the story of the Boo Hag (also called Hag) before my haunting. And so far, I haven't seen her since. The night of my experience was a normal night like any other. I usually go to sleep by midnight or 1 am. I'm more of a night owl than a morning person. I wake up quite frequently, too. This could be caused by any number of things, noises such as the neighbor's dog barking, people leaving the MarshWalk after an evening of food and drink. But, when I awoke that night, for some unknown reason, I could not move. Not an inch. My eyes were wide open but my arms and legs were useless. As I looked to the right side of my bed, a shadow approached me. At first, a thick, black shape, but suddenly, her face appeared. It was that of an old hag. Her hair was thin and wiry. Her skin was a pale gray with huge black eyes. As soon as I saw her, she jumped onto me. My first reaction was to run, but I still could not move. So, I tried to scream for my husband. But with each gasp of air, not a word nor sound left my lips. She was taking each breath from me. I couldn't take air into my lungs. Now, to say I was scared is an understatement. Terrified was more like it.

So, I closed my eyes and prayed to the Archangels and my guides to help me. With that, I was able to kick my legs with every ounce of energy I had. And, she disappeared. I leaped from my bed, turned on the lamp, threw on my robe, and ran into the living room. I never thought I could move that fast! I spent the rest of the night curled up on the sofa, trying to make heads or tails of this ghastly ghost. Why was she attacking me?

The next morning, I decided to investigate who or what this thing was. Over the next few days, I discovered a local Gullah story about a witch that may have lived in our area. It was more a legend than history, of course. But, it was too much of a coincidence that I would experience this witchy spirit and then find out later that there was talk of such a specter.

I had been researching for hours when I decided to take a break. Going through television channels, I came across a show about the paranormal. It was an interview show about real people's ghostly experiences. On the show was a young lady who tells of a hag attacking her in the night. Same looking entity as mine. Same frightful experience. Lack of movement, loss of breath, etc. So, I was happy to know I wasn't alone. I felt bad for the young girl but felt better for myself. I did not imagine her. My experience was real.

So, this is the actual story I found in my research.

The legend tells of a man who marries a local woman. We do not know the year but I figure this story was told well over a hundred years ago. Seems this young man is talking to his neighbor. The neighbor asks how married life is going for him. The gentleman says he is concerned about his new bride. Every night since their marriage, she waits for him to fall asleep, then quietly creeps out of the house. He awakes to find her gone but she always returns before sunrise. The neighbor's jaw drops in disbelief and he tells the gentleman that he has married a boo hag...a witch! The gentleman is astonished. How is this possible? His wife is a beautiful, young woman who has always been kind and sweet-natured. So the neighbor tells him the reason she leaves at night is to attack those in their sleep and inhale their spirit or soul to keep herself alive. When she leaves the house, she takes off her skin and will hide it somewhere near their home. Once she has shed her outer skin, she takes the form of a ghostly hag. She'll fly through the area and find victims at home in their beds. When she has completed feeding on her victims, she must return to her home before sunrise where she will put back on her skin and return to her beautiful, young self.

The gentleman looks toward his neighbor for help. So the neighbor tells him when she leaves at night to find out where she hid her skin and spread salt all over it. This will cause her skin to shrink and make it impossible to get back in. Once the morning sun hits her true ghostly form, she shall disappear.

That night, the gentleman watches secretly as his wife sneaks out the front door. He peeks through the window and watches her take off her skin and place it under the front porch steps. She becomes a horrid, old hag and suddenly disappears into the night. So the man does what he was told. He took her skin and sprinkled salt all over it and replaced it under the porch. He goes back to bed and waits until dawn. Just before the sun rises, he hears his wife out on the porch. He then hears her scream, " Skin, skin let me in!" She repeats the words over and over but she is unable to put her skin on. Seeing the sun about to rise, she rushes into the house to hide under the bedsheets.

Her husband jumps out of bed to confront her, but she pulls the covers tight and tells him to leave. He then grabs the covers off to find the hideous face and body of a witch. He runs to the window and opens the curtains to let the light of the sunshine on her. With an anguished cry, she disappears in a cloud of smoke.

So this is the legend of the Hag. Some will say that the hag is nothing more than just a bad dream or nightmare. But doctors also know of another cause. So I researched a term called sleep paralysis. The affliction causes people to wake from sleep but makes them unable to move. Although their eyes and ears are working, they are paralyzed from the neck down. This is very much like my experience. But, many say as they look around the room, they see an apparition near the bed. In most cases...it's an old witch or hag. She sits on their chest and takes the breath from them. Then it will disappear. Doctors say it is only because your body is still asleep and your mind is only partially awake that you may hallucinate. What is so unusual is they will see an old hag of all things.

Now, I gotta tell you something. If I am going to hallucinate about someone hovering over me, I want it to be George Clooney or some other handsome movie star. Why is it that most people hallucinate about a witch? It seems to be the chosen haunt... but why? It doesn't make sense that so many people across the world have the same hallucination during sleep paralysis.

So, my advice to you is, if you find yourself newly married and your wife disappears in the night, keep plenty of salt by your bedside. You just might need it.

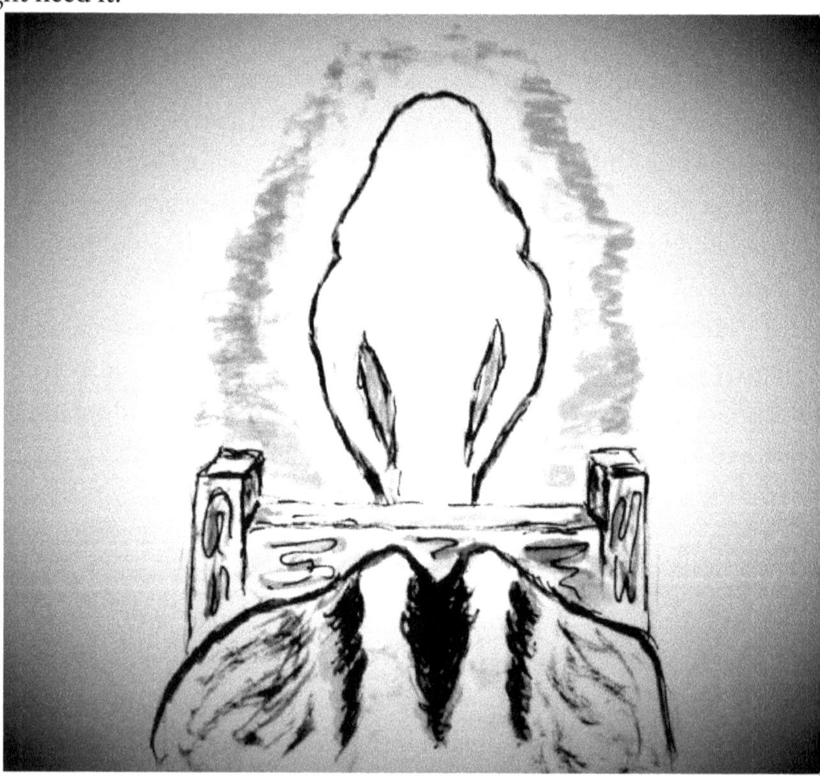

The Ghost Dogs of Pawleys Island

I love dogs. I have owned (or should I say cared for and loved) many dogs over the years. All different breeds, sizes, and personalities. I don't often tell this story on my tours. It is a sad tale to tell. But, it is a tale not too many people have heard. So here we go.

A lovely woman was the caretaker at the Pelican Inn. It is, as I have stated before, one of the oldest homes in Pawleys Island. The caretaker owned two Boston Terriers, whom she utterly adored. She and her dogs would go for long walks along the beach. The dogs would jump, bark and run along the dunes. Many neighbors would hear the dogs run up and down the coast playing in the salty surf.

One day on their daily walk, one of the dogs spotted a young child playing in the surf. The child was overcome by a huge wave and was being pulled out to sea by a powerful riptide. One of the dogs jumped into the water and swam out to the child. The young one grabbed hold of the dog's collar and was pulled into shore safely. Both child and dog lived but soon the terrier would become ill. He had ingested so much saltwater he was losing his battle with life. He died shortly after. The dogs' littermate was sullen with grief. Refusing to eat or drink, the second of the terriers died of a broken heart. The caretaker herself was taken with grief at the loss of her canine companions and never owned another dog again.

It is said that a year or so later, neighborhood children were playing on the beach. Parents heard their children laughing accompanied by what sounded like two dogs barking. Taking a look, they thought for sure it was the same two Boston Terriers who had belonged to the caretaker. But, every time the people would look for the two, all they would find were their paw prints in the sand.

Others have said that the caretaker did see her dogs again. When she was walking the beach on Pawleys Island, she thought she heard a couple of dogs barking behind her. She turned around and was astonished to see what looked like her terriers running towards her. But before they got close to her arms, they softy faded away. The only remains of their visit were their paw prints in the white, beach sand.

I hope the pups are still having a wonderful time playing and frolicking on the island. We do have leash laws on some of our beaches, but I don't think the terriers will be needing them. It is fitting that there be dogs haunting the beach. It is called 'Paw-leys Island, after all.

The Pelican Inn

The history of the Pelican Inn is long and vast being one of a very small number of historical Lowcountry homes that still exist in Pawleys Island, SC. The home was built in the 1840s as the summer home for Hagley Plantation owner, Plowden Charles Jenrette Weston. The Pelican Inn was built behind a tall sand dune and is surrounded by live oaks which helps protect the home from strong winds and tidal surges. This was it's saving grace from hurricanes such as Hugo and Hazel. The home was constructed so that soft, ocean breezes would flow through the windows and doors to cool off visitors during the hot, humid southern summers.

In 1864, the property was sold to William St. Julien Mazyck. He sold the home to the Atlantic Coast Lumber Company in 1901. The Pelican Inn would go through many different owners over the years. It is now run as a bed-n-breakfast.

So, who haunts the Pelican Inn? Well, I've already told the story of the Grey Man. They say it may be Plowden Weston who shows his spectral self in his grey civil war uniform advising people to leave the island due to an impending hurricane. But, as I have stated, the first known sighting of the Grey Man was in 1822. That was long before Plowden Weston died. Some say Plowden's wife, Emily haunts the inn. Some say they smell her sweet lilac perfume as it wafts through the home.

A couple years ago, I emailed the present owner and asked if she had any strange occurrences in or around the home. She told me the spirits are actually playful at the inn. She and her husband would lay an item down on a counter or table, then go back for it and it would be missing. For instance, one day she had poured herself a cup of coffee. She placed it on the counter and only turned away for a moment. When she went to retrieve her cup, it was gone. She looked all around the kitchen and finally found it on top of the refrigerator. No one else was in the home that day and she didn't place the cup upon the frig. She told me she is too short to reach the top.

I recently met a long time resident of the South Strand while writing this book. This was not a chance meeting and more than just a coincidence. He told me he had quite a number of stories regarding the Pelican Inn. Come to find out, he had been the previous caretaker. He told me of the first night he spent all alone at the old inn back in the late 1990's. The owner had asked him to watch the inn for a month while she was out of town. He tells me that the first night was a very long one.

One day, he had asked a group of friends to spend the night. Six men he had known for a number of years. They brought supplies for their stay and were just getting ready to settle down to sleep. The caretaker suddenly heard a commotion and saw all 6 men run out of the inn, most leaving their personal items behind. Not one stopped to say goodbye but ran for their cars and left.

It was sometime later when the caretaker talked to one of the men. He refused to say what startled them so badly. In fact, none of the men would talk about their experience at the old inn. So, I will leave this as a mystery for now. Hopefully, my friend will write about the experience himself. Or, maybe...let me in on the secret someday.

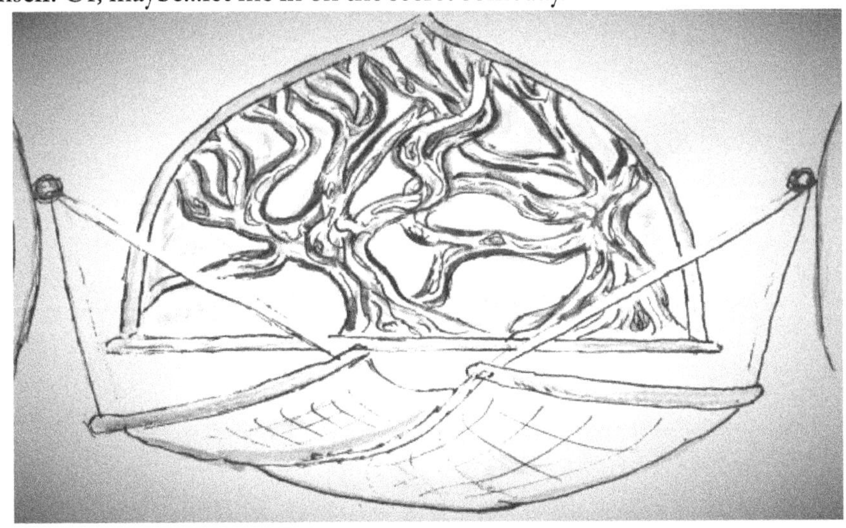

The Grape Vine Legend

What? You never heard of the Grape Vine Legend? Well, I may know why. Because, it is my own personal story regarding Hurricane Matthew and an ugly, old muscadine grapevine that has taken over my yard. It is a massive vine, as thick as my arm and floats throughout my trees. People told me that I should cut it down. They thought this massive old vine was an eyesore to have in my garden. But something always told me the vine was a good thing to have even though it wasn't as lovely as our other plants and flowers. It must have taken many generations to reach that thickness and length. I couldn't bring myself to cut down something that may have been around since the plantation days.

The wind was extremely strong that day back in October of 2016. It was to be my first big hurricane here in Murrells Inlet. I had been through one hurricane before when I lived further north, but this is my first with my husband, Paul.

Paul had been through many hurricanes before including Hugo. He isn't one to get very anxious. He's very laid back and being he lived through Hugo, he said he could make it through any storm. So, we did not evacuate the area. We live but a block from the inlet. During high tides and torrential rain, flooding can become a deadly issue.

Winds were building upwards of 75-80 miles per hour throughout the day. We had a huge sycamore tree in front of our house along with many cedar trees that my husband, Paul, had planted many years before. They were lined up in a row along the northeast side of our home. We purchased a camper a couple years before and placed it beneath the cedars. We spent many hours and dollars restoring the floors and replacing furniture. We had just gotten it finished when Hurricane Matthew made its presence known. As the day continued, the wind got stronger. It was blowing between our neighbors' houses and increased in strength. It was like a wind tunnel blowing through our cedars and the sycamore.

As I looked out my front window, I could see our sycamore being twisted around and around. The winds were so powerful and I thought that being the tree was over 3 stories high, it would win the battle against the winds. But, then I had a feeling that something bad was about to happen. I ran for my cell phone.

Suddenly with a great crack, the 3-story tall sycamore unfortunately, fell into our neighbor's utility pole, snapping it in half. But, at the same moment the sycamore falls, I hear another cracking sound from the northeast corner of our house. I turn to look out the kitchen window and here comes one of the cedar trees slowly falling, root ball and all towards our camper and also, our house. Nervous doesn't explain how I felt. I prayed to God and Spirit for help while yelling to my husband to come and witness what I thought would be the end of our camper and maybe, our home.

But, suddenly, the tree stopped falling. It swung to and fro a few inches, but stopped it's journey into our camper. The winds continued to howl for hours. But the cedar stayed leaning at an unusual angle over the camper. All we could do was watch and wait to see what our fate would be against the storm.

It seemed like an eternity waiting for the winds to subside and the storm to be over. But finally, it was now safe for us to venture out. We were more concerned for our neighbors not having power and wanted to make sure they were okay. We were just grateful all of us were safe. We then turned our attention to the cedar tree. We couldn't understand how the cedar was still leaning at such an angle. Why didn't it fall?

The next morning, a friend of ours who worked in the tree service industry came to inspect our damage and help with cleanup. As he approached our cedar tree, he stopped with a look of wonder on his face. How the tree remained standing on such an angle without falling was the question. As he began to trim away the limbs, we all saw the reason for the miracle. A small grapevine had twisted it's way around the top of the tree and was holding it up for dear life. I told our friend not to cut away too much of the vine but to save what he could of it. I felt I owed it to the vine to cut away as little as possible. The tree was sawed into logs and to this day we still burn them in our firepit.

Cedar is a very spiritual tree. The wood has been used in ceremonies by Native American people for centuries. Cherokee believe that their dead reside in the trees in order to protect their people. I believe between the cedars and the vine, they have a special bond or maybe a job to do. Maybe they are both here to protect us.

Litchfield Plantation

Between Murrells Inlet and Pawleys Island is a tiny community called Litchfield. Surrounded by old, live oaks and wrought iron fencing is a beautiful plantation home. Litchfield Plantation was built prior to the Revolutionary War. The land was originally owned by Thomas Hepworth in 1710. Eventually, the land and plantation home would be named "Litchfield" by Peter Simon.

The home and property had gone through different families over the years, however one family that owned the home in the mid 1850s were the Tuckers. Daniel Tucker was a politician and had three sons. The eldest, Mr. John H. Tucker inherited Litchfield and cared for the house and the grounds. He would have 9 sons by 4 different wives.

When John Tucker died, his son, Dr. Henry M. Tucker inherited the vast plantation. The Tuckers perfected the growing methods of rice and became quite wealthy. But, Dr. Tucker also had a thriving medical practice during and after the Civil War. It is said he would make house calls to many of the other plantations to care for the ill. Being Litchfield was a working plantation, Dr. Tucker had a bell installed on the gate at the end of the long drive lined by huge oak trees. When he would come back home late at night, he would ring the bell and a gatekeeper would open the gate for him. Tucker then rode his horse down 'the avenue of the oaks' and climbed the back staircase to not wake his family. He would die years later at the plantation, but some say he may not have left his beloved home.

I remember the first time hearing the tale of Dr. Tucker. I was sitting on the front porch of a local gift shop called the Lazy Gator. It's a well-known Lowcountry store with a huge porch and plenty of colorful rocking chairs for guests to rest on or just rock the day away. Usually, it's husbands who rock away the time on the porch while their wives shop. The store is located just across from the MarshWalk in Murrells Inlet.

Management allows me to meet and greet my ghost tour guests on their front porch.

This one particular night, I was sitting and giving out information regarding my tour, when an elderly gentleman and his wife walked up the steps and the man sat next to me in one of the rockers. His wife quickly ran in to make her purchases.

The gentleman turned and gave me an odd look. I guess he would, I was dressed in my tour guide outfit as a pirate. I always dress in pirate garb...we did have pirates come to our inlet hundreds of years ago. It also gives folks something to talk about, especially children. When they ask why I dress this way, it gives me the opportunity to tell them a little of our history of piracy, ghosts and local history.

In any case, I turned to the gentleman and explained that I do the local ghost and history tour and that was the reason for the costume. He slowly smiled and said he had a wonderful story for me. A story about the ghost of Litchfield Plantation. He now has my full attention.

He tells me he used to work for the plantation. Litchfield Plantation is now used for weddings and special events. But, he told me there was a time when folks could stay there overnight. He was a custodian of sorts, cleaning up and helping where he could. He tells me one particular night he was sweeping the front hall when he thought he heard the sounds of horses hooves galloping up the avenue of the oaks. He stopped what he was doing and listened quietly for the sound. But, it stopped as fast as it started. Feeling he must have been mistaken, he continued with his chores. It was then that he heard a front door knob rattle, as if someone was trying to force the door open. He knew the doors were locked and thought maybe it was a coworker who was returning to the home because they had forgotten something. Just as he looked out the window, the door knob became quiet and he saw no one outside. He tells me this is when he became a bit nervous, but continued his job. Then, something stopped him in his tracks. The sound of footsteps going up the staircase towards one of the bedrooms. The bedroom of Dr. Henry Tucker.

He then told me he ran out of the home as fast as he could. And, quit his job the next day.

We must have spent 20 minutes talking and exchanging stories, when his wife exited the store. She asked her husband what sort of tales he was telling me about. When he said Litchfield, she also told me that when he got home he was as white as a (excuse the pun) 'ghost' and told her what he had seen. She then verified that he did quit his job because of what he saw. I thanked them both for their amusing tales and watched them walk to their car. I didn't catch their names, but I want to thank them for the great story.

A few other people I interviewed told me their tale as well. I spoke with ladies that had worked there when it was an inn. Folks would call down to the front desk late at night and complain about a bell ringing. The only bell on the property was at the front gate down the avenue. The ladies would then walk down the avenue and look to see who rang the bell. But, they would never find anyone. It got rather bothersome to have to walk down the avenue everytime folks complained about the noise, so the owners decided to take the bell down. But, it didn't matter. People would still complain about the noisy bell ringing late at night.

Another lady would tell me folks complained of a loud party going on outside the building. Guests would tell her of voices mumbling but they couldn't quite understand what was being said. Again, a worker would check. But the staff already knew no one would be found. I also talked to a ghost hunter who brought a digital recorder with him. He hoped to capture a voice or two...and he did. While on the front porch,he heard the voices of men discussing weather and the crops. There were no other people at the home that day.

It seems the home is still very active and, perhaps, Dr. Tucker is still making housecalls, even today.

The Plat-Eye

This is probably one of the most unusual tales I have ever heard. And, I have heard quite a few over the years. This story deals with an animal (or maybe creature is a better term for it). Although I have only heard this story once, I feel it has a place in this book.

In many different cultures from all over the world, including here in America, many tribal members talk about 'shapeshifters'. These creatures start out as a human but slowly change form to become a dangerous beast. In our American Indian culture, many tribal shamans are known to change shape into a wolf, bear or even an eagle. Some say they protect the tribal members while in these animal forms. Others, like the Navajo, for instance, call these creatures 'skinwalkers'. To the Navajo, the skinwalker is dangerous and cunning.

In the Lowcountry, the Gullah Geechee (descendants of freed slaves) have their rendition of a type of shapeshifter. It is called the Plat-eye. It is called this because of its plate sized, red eyes that burn like hot embers. Some believe it is the spirit of someone who worked the local plantation and didn't receive a proper burial. They believe the victims ghost would rise out of the misty marsh to seek revenge. Others say it is that of a murdered slave. Some have heard tales of Confederate soldiers burying treasure here in the area and they would also bury a slave with the treasure so his spirit would guard it for them. Now, if I was murdered by soldiers, I don't think I would be hanging around guarding their gold. Likely, I'd be haunting them instead.

The story begins in the early 1900s. It is said there was a young woman whose ancestors worked the indigo and rice plantations along the Waccamaw River. With her bucket and oyster rake in hand, she walked to the inlet to fetch some oysters. She had gotten a late start and had been warned by her family to come back before sunset. And, under no circumstances, was she to walk through the local graveyard at night. She promised she would hurry and make it home before dark. But, all good intentions die hard. She lost track of time and before she knew it, night was falling. She needed to rush home as fast as possible and knew that the quickest route would be through a local cemetery. The cemetery in Murrells Inlet is quite small, not quite an acre or 2 so she thought no harm could come to her if she ran swiftly down it's narrow path.

She began to run through the cemetery when suddenly, a black cat appeared on the trail and stopped her dead in her tracks. The cat refused to move and let her pass, so the young girl took her oyster rake and poked at the cat. But, to her amazement, the small, black cat rose and turned into a giant black panther with huge, red glowing eyes! She was terrified. As the panther approached her she had no other recourse than to take her rake and stab at the great cat. But, the panther growled at her and, once again, changed its shape. This time, turning into a giant alligator with coal red eyes! Well, she didn't want to take the chance of poking this creature with her rake again, so she gathered up all the courage she could and jumped over the monster. It snapped at her heels, but missed.

Without looking back, she continued to run through the cemetery and back to her family cottage. Once home and quite out of breath, she told her family what she had witnessed. Her family shook their heads. They had warned her about staying out too late at night and taking the path through the cemetery. But, they were glad she was all right.

While investigating this story, I found a special concoction that you should have on you if you expect to go walking in cemeteries late at night in the Murrells Inlet area. Find yourself some flannel cloth and cut it into a large square. Take some gunpowder and some sulfur and tie it up tight in the cloth. Put it in your shirt pocket next to your heart. Now, I don't guarantee it would ward off plat-eyes. But, maybe it's better you don't go walking after midnight in our South Strand graveyards.

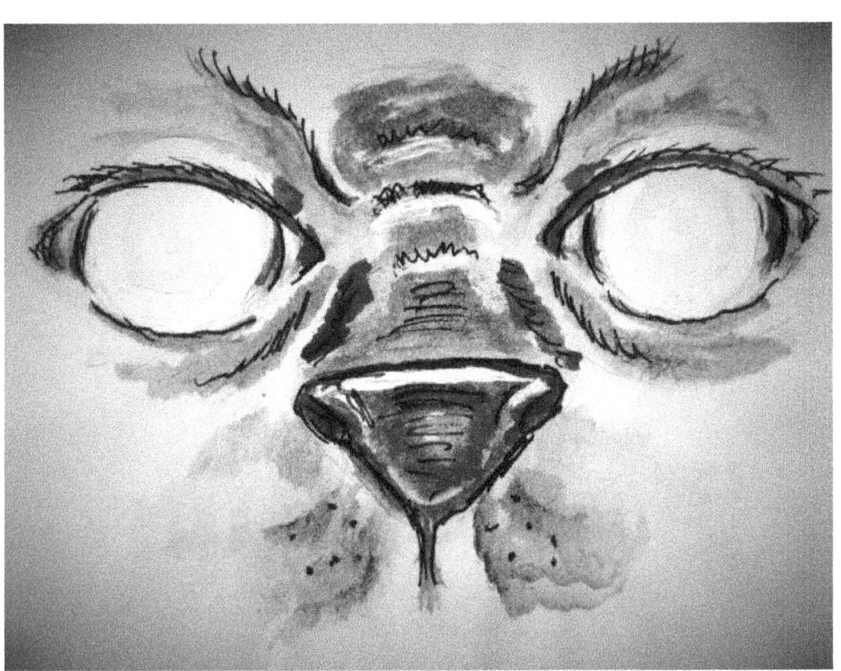

The Crab Boy

The following is a tale by the Gullah, whom I mentioned before are the descendants of freed slaves in our area. These are the folks who know the region well. They know the ins and outs of fishing, clamming and gathering oysters for their families. It is the life's blood here on the inlet. But, another favorite shellfish along our coast are crabs. Today, folks mostly indulge in blue crabs. Blue crabs are easier to obtain compared to walking through pluff mud with shovels and pails. Taking a crab trap with a couple pieces of raw chicken inside and tossing it into the water usually works wonders.

But, there was a time in the early 1900s when locals enjoyed another type of crab. The ghost crab. These crabs are very pale in color. They live in burrows on our beaches. There is only one way to catch them, and it isn't much fun. You must find the largest burrow on the beach, roll up your sleeve and very carefully reach in and feel your way around for the crab's claw. If you are lucky enough, you will find the claw before it finds your fingers. Grab the claw as fast as you can, twist it around and pull out the crab. You must be quick or you could lose a finger or two.

So, the story goes, a young boy was visiting his family in the inlet. He was raised near the city and was not versed in the ways of crabbing. He spent most of the day watching his cousins and other relatives walk along the beach grabbing up ghost crabs for their dinner. Once they felt they had enough for their meal, the group returned to the house to prepare their feast. But, the boy felt he had been left out. They wouldn't allow him to put his tiny hand into the burrows. He was still too young, they told him.

The child was not happy being told he was too young. He felt he could go crabbing all by himself. He didn't need anyones help. So, without saying a word, he slips away and runs toward the beach. He finds a huge burrow and knows this is the perfect place for a crab to be hiding. He reaches inside, feels around and suddenly is met with a terrible crushing pain. The crab had clamped down on his tiny fingers and the young boy could not release his hand from the crab's stronghold.

He begins to cry and yells for help. The winds were picking up and were carrying his voice up and down the beach. The sun was already beginning to set. It would be very difficult to find him in the darkness. His family heard his cries for help and ran out toward the beach. They could hear his cries, and continued to look, but did not locate him until the morning. The young boy had drowned. While the young child's hand was trapped in the hole, a high tide came in and swept his poor soul away. Today, they say if you walk around Huntington Beach State Park on a windy night, you may still hear the Crab Boy, crying...help me...help me!

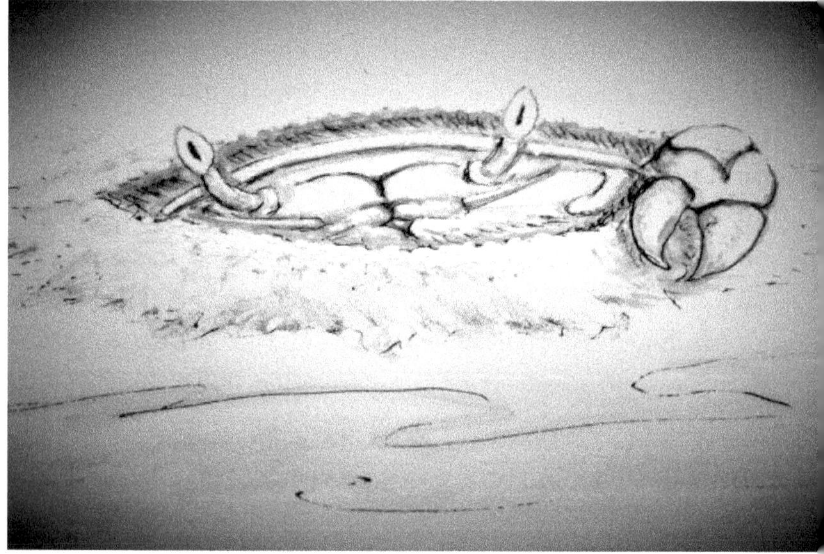

Theodosia Burr Alston

This was one of the greatest mysteries of the early 1800s. The disappearance of Theodosia Burr Alston, the first lady of South Carolina. You may recognise her name if you are a history buff. She was the daughter of Aaron Burr, Vice President of the United States during Thomas Jefferson's presidency.

Theodosia was born in New York in June,1783. Her mother, unfortunately, would not be with her child for long and would pass away when her daughter was only 10. Aaron and his daughter were extremely close and she had the best education and upbringing. In her teen years, she would meet Joseph Alston, a rice plantation owner from Murrells Inlet, SC and soon they wed. She moved to Murrells Inlet to his plantation home, The Oaks, but had a very difficult time dealing with mosquitoes and the humid climate along the Waccamaw River. She would spend most of the summers staying with family near the beach where the breeze was cooler and to get away from the insects. A year later, she and Joseph had a son, Aaron Burr Alston. The birth was hard on Theodosia and her health. She would never be able to have more children.

But, in 1812, what should have been her happiest year was her saddest. Although her husband had just been named Governor of South Carolina and she would receive the title of first lady, she would lose her only child, Aaron. She was grief stricken and felt all alone. Her husband was away from home more often due to political reasons. Her father had just returned to New York from his 'self-imposed' exile after the end of his political career and his failed plot to take over Mexico. Aaron Burr asked his daughter to come back north and he would take care of her. She and Joseph thought this a good idea and he acquired a schooner called the Patriot to take her to New York. The ship left from Georgetown harbor and Theodosia Burr Alston would disappear in the first days of 1813.

Many thought the ship had been destroyed by the British Navy. We were engaged in the War of 1812, but there are no records of the British attacking the ship at sea. Some say the ship was boarded by pirates and poor Theodosia was forced to walk the plank. It is said that 3 different pirates confessed on their deathbeds that they were the one who forced Theodosia to walk the plank to her watery grave. Historically speaking, pirates didn't make people walk the plank. In all of pirate history, there is only one maybe two times I have ever read about this. It's more a Hollywood legend than real life.

Others say she married a pirate captain and sailed away towards the Gulf of Mexico.

Finally, some believe it was the wreckers that got her. The wreckers were a group of people who lived on the North Carolina coast along the passage they named the 'Graveyard of the Atlantic'. These 'land pirates' would place lanterns along the rocky coast to trick ships in the night to believe it was a harbor. The ships would crash upon the reef and the locals would run onto the ship, kill everyone and steal everything onboard. Then, the ship would sink and the ocean itself would cover up any sign of a crime.

Still, many of us believe (I, myself included) it was a great storm that took the lives of the Patriot. The weather was rough that time of year and this is probably the best answer to the mystery.

But, where does Theodosia still haunt? She is quite busy according to locals and vacationers I have talked to. Some say she haunts the area now known as Brookgreen Gardens where her and Joseph's home, The Oaks once stood. Others have told me they have seen a figure in white along what is now called Litchfield Beach, just south of Murrells Inlet. It was said Theodosia spent time at her father-in-laws home on that beach when the summer heat approached. I have seen a couple of photos from my tour guests showing a wispy white form flowing down the sand. I had one guest tell me how he was vacationing in Litchfield and while walking the beach, he saw a white mist flow past him. He says it had the form of a woman in a flowing gown. But, before he could take a photo, she was gone. Still, others say in a town called Georgetown, Theodosia may haunt a friend's home where she stayed just before her infamous voyage. And then, there is the Harborwalk in that same town. It is a small boardwalk that links restaurants together along the river. They say it is where she said her last good-bye to her husband before boarding the ill-fated ship.

It seems Theodosia Burr Alston had an amazingly, incredible life and an equally incredible, mysterious death.

Bibliography

"*All Saints Church-Waccamaw*" - Henry D. Bull-The Reprint Co.,Publishers 1994

"*Ghosts From The Coast*" - Julian S. Bolick-The Presses of Jacob Brothers

Copyright 1966

"*Heaven Is a Beautiful Place*"- Genevieve C. Peterkin- University of South Carolina Press-Copyright 2000

"*Musings of a Hermit*"- Clarke A. Willcox-Walker,Evans & Cogswell Co.-Copyright 1966

"*Tales Along The King's Highway of South Carolina*"- Blanche W. Floyd-Bandit Books Copyright 1999

"*Theodosia Burr Alston*'- Richard N. Cote'-Corinthian Books-Copyright 2003

"*Waccamaw Plantations*"-Julian S. Bolick-Jacobs Press -Copyright 1946

Cover Illustration created by Christine Vernon

Story Illustrations created by Christine Vernon

Don't miss out!

Visit the website below and you can sign up to receive emails whenever Christine Vernon publishes a new book. There's no charge and no obligation.

https://books2read.com/r/B-A-ISWM-GQBLB

BOOKS 2 READ

Connecting independent readers to independent writers.

About the Author

Christine (Wannop) Vernon grew up in a suburb of Phila, PA. She spent many years studying both fine arts as well as live theater. She moved to South Carolina in 2005 and began investigating the history and legends of the South Strand. She currently sells her original artwork at her home studio and lectures at museums, universities, and local venues. She owns/operates Miss Chris' Inlet Walking Tour-a local ghost and history tour on the Murrells Inlet MarshWalk.

Read more at https://www.facebook.com/inletcottageandwalkingtour.

www.ingramcontent.com/pod-product-compliance
Ingram Content Group UK Ltd.
Pitfield, Milton Keynes, MK11 3LW, UK
UKHW022007190726
13853UKWH00004B/1789